WHAT'S A
SYNTHESIZER?
Simple Answers to Common Questions

by Jon F. Eiche

revised by Emile Menasché

HAL•LEONARD®
CORPORATION

7777 W. BLUEMOUND RD. P.O. BOX 13819 MILWAUKEE, WI 53213

ISBN 0-634-01344-0

HAL•LEONARD®
CORPORATION

7777 W. BLUEMOUND RD. P.O. BOX 13819 MILWAUKEE, WI 53213

Visit Hal Leonard Online at
www.halleonard.com

CONTENTS

Preface v

Introduction 1

1. What's a Synthesizer? 3
   Sound Waves 4
   Pitch 5
   Volume 7
   Timbre 9

2. The Roots of Synthesis 11
   Pitch 12
   Volume 13
   Timbre 15
   Modulation 16
   Putting It All Together 18

3. Making Sound Come to Life 19
   Controllers 20
   Other Elements 23
   Voices 24
   Microprocessor Control 25

4. How Does Digital Synthesis Work? 27
   Algorithms 28
   Physical Modeling 31
   Sample Playback Synths 31
   Software Synths 32
   Computer-Based Hardware Synths 32

5. Why Is Digital Sampling So Popular? 34
   Multi-Sampling 35
   Looping 37
   Resynthesis 37

6. **What Do All Those Other Boxes Do?** **39**

    Effects. 39

    Instruments 41

7. **What Is MIDI?** **44**

    What MIDI Is. 45

    What MIDI Does 45

    General MIDI. 49

    More Than Notes 50

    System Exclusive. 50

    MIDI Implementation Chart. 51

    The Computer Connection 52

Coda **54**

Glossary **55**

Index **56**

About the Authors **58**

PREFACE

OVER THE LAST DECADE, electronic music has undergone a massive transformation. Once the domain of experimental music, electronic musical devices — better known as synthesizers, samplers, drum machines, sequencers — have become more accessible, better sounding, easier to understand, and more useful than ever before. In the process, they have taken over many genres of the music industry.

When the first edition of *What's a Synthesizer?* appeared, analog synths still dominated the scene, digital synthesizers were just coming into prominence, and 8- and 12-bit samplers were state of the art. A lot has changed since then: new forms of digital synthesis have emerged that are more flexible their predecessors; samplers routinely record at CD-quality or better; and computers have come to dominate the composition and production of music. In the process, various synthesis techniques have come in and out of prominence: A few years ago, you couldn't give away an old analog synth. Now, the same device may well fetch a king's ransom. In fact, the emulation and expansion of analog sounds is a key selling point of today's digital synths.

So although the answer to the question, What's a synthesizer? certainly has changed over the years, the principles outlined by Jon Eiche in the original volume remain true today. You may not use a real analog synth and you may not have an old FM module in the closet. But as you sit down in front of a sleek, new music machine, knowing how the original devices worked will help get you past the presets and make the sound your own.

—Emile Menasché

INTRODUCTION

Do you need a Ph.D. in electrical engineering?

UNLESS YOU'VE SPENT the last 30 years in a cave or on a desert island, you're aware that the march of technology has accelerated to a run. This has affected all areas of our lives, though perhaps none so strikingly as music. The new musical technology — **electronic** technology — has amounted to nothing less than a revolution. Portable keyboards, for example, didn't even exist until the early 1980s. When they first came out, they were regarded as expensive toys. But by their sheer and unprecedented popularity, they have taken their place among "legitimate" musical instruments. Computers have also played a role in transforming the way we make, listen to, and distribute music.

Even the tradition-bound world of Bach and Mozart has been affected. Interestingly, the electronic revolution transformed classical music even before pop music. The opening fanfares of this brave-new-world symphony were sounded in 1968, when Wendy Carlos's *Switched-On Bach* first appeared in record bins. This one recording — realized entirely on a Moog synthesizer — and which sold more copies than any classical recording ever had before, proved to a disbelieving world that electronics could indeed produce *music*. Since then, use of electronic musical instruments by professional and amateur musicians alike has increased at an enormous rate. Today, almost all pop music incorporates some form of synthesis.

Today, synthesizers, portable keyboards, drum machines, and samplers populate the world of electronic musical instruments. This fertile ground of instruments and new ideas has stimulated crossbreeding between these species. The distinctions between them become fuzzier by the day. For example, portable keyboards, which initially borrowed heavily from electronic organs, have steadily taken on the characteristics of synthesizers. As technology evolves, new levels of sound design and control become available, affording players and composers more power than ever before to push the sonic envelope.

Another by-product of new musical technology is that equipment (that does more than it ever did before) costs *less* than ever before. Professional-caliber instruments are within reach of the nonprofessional pocketbook. What's more, technology has elevated the mind and the ear to positions of greater importance than mere manual dexterity, opening the riches of music making to those formerly denied access. This "democratization of music," as it has been called, is a dream come true for many would-be musicians. Perhaps you are one of them.

If there is a problem with any of this, it is the problem of ignorance and confusion. There seems to be so much to learn and you're afraid that it may be overwhelming. Never fear. You *can* learn enough to enjoy using this new musical technology, and you *don't* need a Ph.D. in electrical engineering to do so. This book will get you started.

Whether you are cautious and skeptical or curious and enthusiastic, you'll find answers to your questions here. The pages that follow constitute a brief, understandable overview of the world of electronic sound. Things are kept simple enough so that you won't get lost, but you are told enough so that, should you wish to ask even more questions, you'll know *how* to ask them.

1.
WHAT'S *A SYNTHESIZER?*

THE WORD "SYNTHESIZE" means "to put together." In musical parlance, the term has become very broad. Synthesis, once limited to analog circuits using oscillators and filter circuitry, now encompasses a broad range of technologies. This runs the gamut from analog (and digital synthesis that emulates analog performance), to various types of digital synthesis, to digital sampling, to software-based physical modeling. While the technology has changed over the years, many of the principles developed in early synthesizers remain with us today.

Modern day synths are powerful music production tools, capable of playing (and recording) many simultaneous voices independent from one another (multitimbral operation), mixing them internally (often with built-in effects), and outputting the results to a finished product. A synthesizer is a device that puts together the elements that make up a sound. So, in attempting to understand synthesizers, you must spend a little time getting to know what sound is about. Think about it for a moment: what is it that makes one sound different from another?

- How can you tell the difference between a tuba and P a piccolo?

- What distinguishes a whisper from a yell? A

- Why does a saxophone sound different from a violin? T

3

There are many subtle things that distinguish the sounds in the examples above. Our ears can hear an astounding range of little differences, which is why it's possible to identify so many distinct sounds. But let's concentrate on the obvious for now:

- A tuba note is **lower** than a piccolo note; this is a difference in **pitch**.

- A whisper is **softer** than a yell; this is a difference in (volume.) *amp*.

- A saxophone sounds, well, **different** than a violin, even if they play the same pitches at the same volume. This is a difference in **timbre** (pronounced "*tam*-ber"), or tone color. While it's a little harder to define, at least at first, than differences in volume or pitch, it's just as clear to our ears.

The three properties outlined in these three examples are the building blocks of all sound. These are the things that a synthesizer "puts together" in order to make different sounds. Now for a closer look.

Sound Waves

Have you ever stood next to a quiet pond and tossed a stone in, just to watch the smooth surface of the water break into a series of ripples? Sure you have. Think about exactly what happened: When the stone hit the pond, it upset more than just the water immediately around it, because *that* water in turn disturbed the 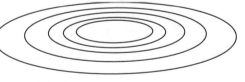 water around *it* — and so on. The result was a series of ripples that spread out in ever-widening circles.

Sound is like that stone and the air is like that pond. When something makes a sound, what it really does is vibrate. You have felt this if you have ever held your hand to your throat while speaking. That vibration causes a disturbance in the air, which spreads outward in ever-widening circles until it reaches your ear. Inside your ear, the disturbance in the air causes the eardrum to vibrate. That vibration is transmitted by an intricate array of connections to a set of nerve endings, which send a message to your brain that you interpret as, "I hear something."

It's not a coincidence that we refer to **sound waves**, a term that brings to mind a picture similar to the ripples in the pond. In a real sense, sound does consist of waves in the air — oscillations of high and low pressure. By connecting a microphone to a device called an **oscilloscope**, it is possible to see a picture of such sound waves.

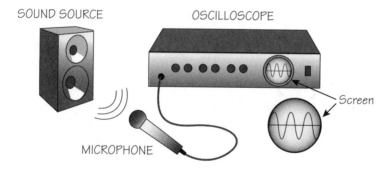

Looking at the picture on the oscilloscope screen, it is easy to grasp what happens in a sound wave: the air pressure alternately rises and falls repeatedly over time.

Pitch

Each repetition of a sound wave is called a **cycle**. The speed at which these cycles occur is called the **frequency** of the wave and is measured, logically enough, in "cycles per second."

If you've ever driven a car, or a motorcycle, or ridden in a motorboat, or operated an electric mixer in your kitchen, you have observed that the sound a motor produces changes depending on how fast it goes. Specifically, the faster a motor runs, the higher the pitch it produces. Motors, like sound waves, operate by making a series of repeated motions — cycles. A faster speed means more cycles per second. More cycles per second means a higher frequency. And, as your ears tell you when you step on the gas pedal in your car, a higher frequency means a higher pitch.

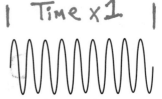

Low Frequency = Low Pitch   High Frequency = High Pitch

"Cycles per second," by the way, is often abbreviated "c.p.s." Another name for the same measurement is "Hertz," often abbreviated "Hz." It was coined in honor of Heinrich Hertz, a 19th-century German physicist who did pioneering work in the field of electromagnetic waves. One advantage of "Hertz" and "Hz" is that they lend themselves well to abbreviation; 1,000 Hertz, for example, can be written as 1 kiloHertz (1kHz), since "kilo-" is the standard scientific abbreviation for "thousand."

The human ear can hear frequencies between about 20Hz (20 cycles per second) and 20kHz (20,000 cycles per second). Below 20Hz, the cycles are heard as separate events and fail to "blur together" as a pitched sound. Above 20kHz, the waves simply move too fast for our ears to respond to. Dog whistles take advantage of a dog's ability to hear higher sounds than we can. The upper limit of human hearing tends to decline with age and with prolonged exposure to loud noise.

The following illustration shows the frequencies of some of the notes on a standard 88-key piano keyboard. Middle C is 261.6Hz. The A above it, sometimes called "concert A" or "A-440," is 440Hz. Every octave higher you go, you double the frequency (the A above A-440 has a frequency of 880Hz); every octave down you go, you halve the frequency.

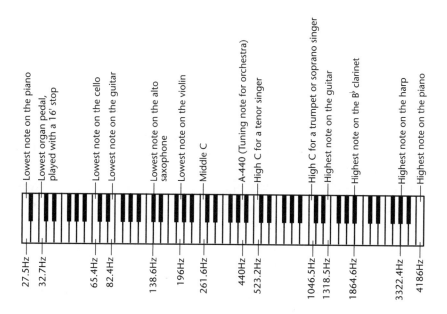

Volume

Now that you've mastered the horizontal dimension of the oscilloscope screen — frequency — you're ready to move on to the vertical dimension. The height of a wave, from top to bottom, is called "amp-litude." It's related to the word "amplifier," and it pertains to **volume**.

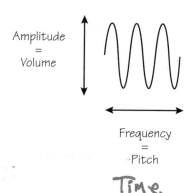

Amplitude
=
Volume

Frequency
=
Pitch

Time

It's easy to understand why this is so: If something makes a small vibration, it creates only a small disturbance in the air. That small disturbance only vibrates our eardrum a little, and so we perceive it as a sound of low volume. But if something makes a big vibration, the disturbance of the air is large. It really rattles our eardrums, and the message to the brain is clear: "LOUD."

Low Amplitude = Soft   High Amplitude = Loud

Just as Hertz is the unit of measurement for frequency, so there is also a unit of measurement for volume: the decibel, abbreviated **dB**. Like Hertz, the decibel is named for a scientist: Alexander Graham Bell. Actually, the full unit of measurement is called a Bel; but since this unit was considered too large for the purposes of discussing the volumes of ordinary sounds, the decibel — a tenth of a Bel — was born.

It is worth noting a subtle distinction between Hertz and decibel: while Hertz is an objective measurement of an aspect of a wave (frequency), the decibel is a subjective measurement of the sound (loudness). Why is this so? Why not talk about measurements of amplitude, the actual height of a sound wave? Because it would be virtually meaningless.

Think about it: A jet plane produces "tall" sound waves. If you were standing on the runway next to a jet starting its engines, you would agree that it's loud. That's why the people who work around planes wear protection for their ears. But after the plane has taken off and is miles away in a matter of seconds, it's not so loud any more. Are the engines putting out smaller vibrations? No; they're just farther away. The moral of the story is, loudness is a relative matter. *not when it is measured*

Let's put loudness on a scale we can understand, as we did with frequency. Zero dB is called the "threshold of hearing"; it represents the softest sound you can hear. At the other end of the scale is the "threshold of pain" — sound so loud that it literally hurts—which is about 120dB.

120dB	Threshold of pain; loud rock music
110dB	Air hammer
100dB	Heavy traffic
90dB	Loud truck
80dB	Full orchestra playing loudly
70dB	String orchestra playing loudly
60dB	Noisy office
50dB	Normal conversation
40dB	Full orchestra playing quietly
30dB	Quiet traffic
20dB	Whispering
10dB	Lightly rustling leaves
0dB	Threshold of hearing; virtual silence

Timbre

So far we've dealt with two of the three properties of sound that were set forth at the beginning of this chapter: pitch and volume. And between them, they use up both dimensions of the oscilloscope screen: horizontal and vertical. Timbre is the aspect of sound that remains to be discussed, but it may not be clear where it fits into the picture. The answer lies in the *shape* of the wave — which is called, logically enough, the **waveshape**, or **waveform**.

The details of how different waveforms correspond to different timbres are beyond the scope of this book. For the purposes of this discussion, it is enough to state a simple truth: a waveform with gentle curves will produce a sound with a somewhat dull, gentle timbre; a waveform with sharp corners will produce a sound with a bright, "sharp" timbre.

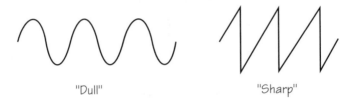

"Dull"   "Sharp"

Differences in timbre and waveform are the results of different **harmonics**, or **overtones**, in sounds. What are harmonics? Well, when you play a note on just about any musical instrument, what you hear is not actually a single tone, but a combination of different ones at different pitches and volumes. These are harmonics, and they are what enable you to tell a saxophone sound from a violin sound. Each musical instrument produces its own characteristic waveform (timbre), the result of a specific combination of harmonics — a "sonic fingerprint" that identifies it to the ear.

By the way, differences in timbre are also what enable us to understand human speech. This is what happens: The vocal cords produce a sound that is rich in harmonics. As the positions of our lips, tongue, and jaw change in forming syllables, they affect the relative volumes of those harmonics, strengthening some and weakening others. The results are audibly different vowel and consonant sounds.

relative level of harmonics

2.
THE ROOTS OF SYNTHESIS

THE BIRTH OF THE SYNTHESIZER came as musicians and electronics engineers pondered a practical way to create and control sound — specifically, to control the three elements of pitch, volume, and timbre. What arose from these ponderings was a collection of related electronic devices, each of which performed a specific task. Originally, each of these devices was a separate module, so the synthesizers were called "modular." These modules were provided with some degree of control, and could be connected in various ways, giving them a certain amount of flexibility.

Connections between modules were made with "patch cords," and the results were called "patches" — terms borrowed from radio and telephone communications. The terminology has proven to be durable, for today, even though few synthesizers use patch cords any more, the control settings for a synth sound are still called a "patch." Since about 1970, more and more synthesizers have been manufactured as self-contained units rather than as collections of modules, trading flexibility for convenience. Nevertheless, the idea of separate, specialized functions remains. *Patch Change Message*

Although digital technology has largely taken over the electronic music world, many of the methods for dealing with sound, and the terminology used to describe those methods, have roots in analog synthesis.

Analog synthesis remains the best place to begin learning about the use of electronics in music, for at least three reasons:

- It is important historically as the starting point of new musical technology.

- It divides synthesis into logical areas that are directly related to the three components of sound (oscillator=pitch, filter=timbre, amplifier=volume).

- Because of reasons 1 and 2 above, many digital synthesizers are patterned after the classic analog model. And analog synthesizers themselves have refused to die out completely.

Pitch

Since sound consists of waves, the basic component in the modular synthesizer is a wave-maker, called an **oscillator**. To further define its operation, it bears the full name **voltage-controlled oscillator,** or **VCO.**

The abbreviation is just one of many spawned in the early years of synthesis; but the meaning is more important than the letters. Control of this module, and all others, is provided by changes of voltage — electricity. The waves that are produced by the oscillator are nothing more than variations in voltage. They are the electrical **analogs** — counterparts — of sound waves that travel through the air. Because the synthesizer produces and manipulates these electrical analogs directly, this kind of synthesis is called **analog synthesis.**

Some kinds of controllers, usually a keyboard, provide a control voltage to the oscillator, telling it what note to play. The earliest synthesizers could only play one note at a time. In the language of synthesis, they were **monophonic. Polyphonic** synthesizers, those capable of playing several notes at a time, were a later development. Most synthesizers now being made are polyphonic, though many have a monophonic mode, which is useful in certain circumstances and styles of music, especially dance genres.

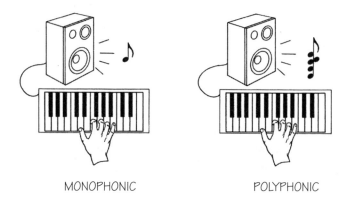

MONOPHONIC   POLYPHONIC

Early polyphonic instruments offered only a few simultaneous voices. More recently, models allowing 64 or even 128 simultaneous voices have become common. You'd have to be an octopus to play all those voices with your fingers, but you'd be surprised how quickly they can be used when the synth is operating in layer and multitimbral modes.

└→ simultaneously

Volume

With the means to produce electrical waves and control pitch, the next component to consider is the one that controls volume. This is the **voltage-controlled amplifier,** or **VCA.** The "voltage-controlled" part is as important here as in the voltage-controlled oscillator. Most musical sounds do not maintain a uniform volume for their entire length; rather, different sounds have different contours, or **envelopes.** A few examples from the world of acoustic instruments illustrate this:

- An accordion note begins slowly because it takes time for the reeds to start vibrating. It builds to a certain level of volume, where it remains for as long as the key is held down and air is being squeezed through the bellows.

- A xylophone note starts quickly and fades away quickly.

- A piano note starts quickly and fades out gradually as long as the key is held down. When the key is released, the note ends quickly.

The synthesizer needs a means to produce different envelopes; the component that provides this means is the **envelope generator.** It allows the synthesizer player to establish the contour of the sound as a series of control voltages that regulate the voltage-controlled amplifier.

The most common envelope generator found in analog synthesizers divides the envelope into four different segments that can be controlled by the synthesist: **Attack, Delay, Sustain,** and **Release.** For this reason, this kind of envelope generator is usually called an **ADSR.**

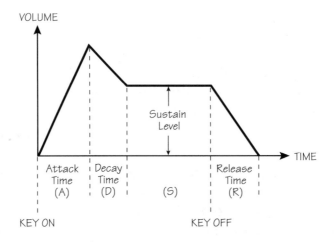

The attack segment governs the time it takes for the level to rise from 0 to an initial peak. Since many envelopes of acoustic sounds decay somewhat after the initial peak, the envelope generator includes a decay segment; as is the case with the attack segment, it controls a length of time. The decay segment ends at the sustain level, which is the level at which the sound remains for as long as the key is held down. After the key is released, the level returns to 0 at a rate determined by the release segment.

The keyboard sends a signal to the envelope generator to start the envelope. This signal, called a **trigger**, is sent when a key is pressed. Another signal, called a **gate**, tells the envelope generator to keep running until the key is released. The gate really *is* the electrical counterpart of gate in a fence: it stays open (on) while the key is down. When the key is released, the gate closes, signaling the envelope generator to begin the release segment of the envelope.

Here's a diagram of the elements covered so far. As is the convention in block diagrams of synthesizers, arrows entering a block from below represent control voltages, and those entering from the left represent audio signals.

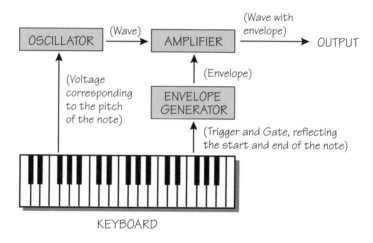

KEYBOARD

Timbre

A typical oscillator in an analog synthesizer offered a choice of several different waveforms for the production of different timbres. These waveforms were all simple shapes and thus easy to produce as patterns of changing voltage. Yet they offered a broad variety of tone colors. Modern digital synths often substitute more complex waveforms, like the ones generated by samples, for these basic waves, but the principle is the same.

Further control over timbre is given by the **voltage-controlled filter**, or **VCF**. Like filters in the physical world, it screens out some elements while letting others pass. What it screens out are harmonics, which you may remember from Chapter 1. Because of the central role played by the filter in the removal of harmonics, analog synthesis is also known as subtractive synthesis.

The filter can be controlled by an envelope generator, just as the amplifier can. In this way, the timbre of a synthesized sound can change over time as the envelope generator changes the extent to which harmonics are filtered out. One example of this, so familiar that is has become a cliché, is the "wow" sound that is perhaps the sound most readily associated with the synthesizer.

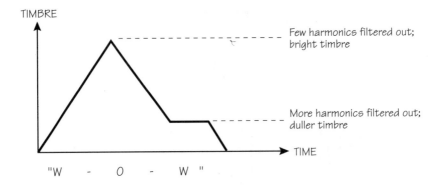

Modulation

The typical synthesizer contains other components designed to provide control over the sound. The most important of these is the **low-frequency oscillator**, or **LFO**. As its name implies, it produces waves at slow speeds (low frequencies) — usually below the audio range. It is used to change the output of the other components (oscillator, amplifier, filter). This kind of change is called **modulation**. When the low-frequency oscillator is used to control the main audio-frequency oscillator, it results in **vibrato**, or **frequency modulation**, which is a repeating variation in pitch. You've probably seen a violinist produce vibrato by moving his or her left hand back and forth on a string while playing. Vibrato often makes a synthesized voice sound more natural.

When the low-frequency oscillator is used to control the amplifier, the result is **tremolo**, or **amplitude modulation**. This is a repeating variation in volume. The most familiar examples of tremolo are the rotating speakers used with electric organs, and the motorized "fans" found on vibraphones.

The low-frequency oscillator can also be used to control the filter, which is simply called **filter modulation**. This is similar to a harmonica player wiggling his hand across the back of his instrument, creating an alternation between a muted and unmuted sound.

The low-frequency oscillator has two basic controls: speed and depth. They correspond to the frequency and the amplitude of the low-frequency wave. Since the latter control is especially useful in performance to add and remove modulation, it is included on many keyboard synthesizers as a small wheel. It is placed at the left end of the keyboard and can be rotated by the thumb or fingers of the left hand while playing. It's usually called the **modulation wheel**, or **mod wheel**.

Other continuous controllers can be used as well. The most popular include channel and polyphonic aftertouch (where adding extra pressure to the key modifies the sound), foot control, and various control sliders, strips, and knobs. (See Chapter 3.)

Putting It All Together

Here is a block diagram of the main components of the analog-type synthesizer as it has been outlined on the previous pages. Be aware that this actually represents only the minimum standard components of a typical synthesizer. Many synthesizers, for example, have the capability of combining two or more audio-frequency oscillators to produce a sound. But what is covered here is enough to give you a solid fundamental understanding of how synthesizers work.

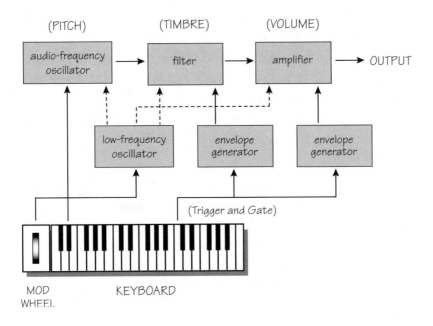

3.

MAKING SOUND COME TO LIFE

BEFORE THE ADVENT of voltage-controlled synthesizers, an earlier generation of electric and electronic instruments, such as the Hammond organ and the Rhodes electric piano, had been developed with the intent of providing economical and, in some cases, portable alternatives to traditional instruments. The sounds of these instruments were, at best, approximations of their acoustic counterparts. In fact, their most prominent features were their idiosyncrasies and shortcomings: a noticeable click at the beginning of each note in the case of the Hammond, and a thick, bell-like timbre in the Rhodes.

Then something odd happened. Over the course of years of being played in concerts and on recordings, the "Hammond sound" and the "Rhodes sound" (to remain with these two examples) became desirable. When the Hammond Organ Company changed the technology in its instruments and did away with the previously unavoidable "key click," many performers were outraged. Public demand forced the company to find a way to "put the click back" into later instruments.

There is a parallel between these earlier instruments and the synthesizer. Although the designers of the modular synthesizers of the 1960s didn't conceive of them for the purpose of imitating acoustic instruments, performers soon began seeking ways to make the synthesizer an imitative instrument. The sounds they developed, though they were poor imitations, became trademarks, so to speak, of the "synthesizer sound." And when newer, digital synthesizers were developed (see Chapter 4), they were judged on their ability to reproduce sounds such as "analog strings" and "synth brass" — as well as, not surprisingly, the Hammond organ and the Rhodes electric piano.

Controllers

Whether synthesizer designers and players agreed on imitative synthesis or not, both groups saw the need to make synthesizers **expressive,** in order to make them true **musical** instruments. This has already been seen in the discussion of envelope generators in Chapter 2. So the designers developed a number of different kinds of controllers to make this possible.

Since most synthesizers are played from a keyboard, it was natural that on many of them the keyboard was given a sensitivity to touch similar to that of the most familiar keyboard instrument: the piano. This kind of touch-sensitivity is called **velocity** sensitivity, for changes in sound are a result of the **speed** with which the key is pressed.

Another kind of touch-sensitivity is **after-touch,** or **pressure** sensitivity. This allows the player to control the sound after the key has been pressed, while it is being held down.

Complete control over the pitch is essential to expressiveness on most acoustic instruments. A guitarist or a clarinetist shapes the pitch of a note every bit as carefully as he or she does the volume or the timbre. Consequently, nearly every keyboard synthesizer includes a controller to obtain pitches that the keyboard alone cannot. This is the **pitch-bend** control. It may take any number of physical forms, including a wheel (similar to the modulation wheel), a lever, a joystick, or a touch-sensitive ribbon. The pitch-bend control is usually near the modulation wheel at the left end of the keyboard; together, these are often referred to as the **left-hand controllers.**

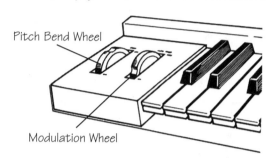

Pitch Bend Wheel

Modulation Wheel

Another means of controlling pitch is **portamento,** sometimes called **glide.** This is usually used in monophonic mode (when the synthesizer can only play one note at a time). It works this way: When the player connects the notes — pressing each successive key down before releasing the previous one — the pitch slides from the former note to the latter one. But when he or she plays the notes separately, they sound separately, with no slide between them. A control on the synth governs the speed of the portamento.

Wind controllers are another class of control devices. The simplest of these are small mouthpieces that connect by wire to the synthesizer and respond to breath pressure. Both hands are left free to play the keyboard and operate other controllers. More elaborate wind controllers are not so much supplements to the keyboard as alternatives to it. The most famous of these is the Lyricon, which looks like — and is played — as a soprano saxophone. There are also trumpetlike wind controllers. In all these cases, the synthesizer itself is separate from the controller.

The idea of separating the control of the synthesizer from the electronics is one that exerted a strong appeal to keyboard players in rock bands during the 1970s. Hidden behind increasingly large stacks of instruments, they envied the freedom of the guitarists to move about the stage and capture the attention of the audience.

Consequently, a few adventuresome players began using portable "strap-on" keyboard controllers. And it should come as little surprise that some of these players, such as Jan Hammer, became known for a style of playing that imitated the guitar, especially in its use of the pitch-bend control. (This serves to make an important point about imitative synthesis: Convincing imitation depends as much on duplicating the playing style of an instrument as it does on reproducing the timbre.)

Once synthesists began pretending they were guitarists, it wasn't long before guitarists wanted to be synthesists. Guitar controllers existed during the 1970s, but it wasn't until MIDI arrived in the 1980s (see Chapter 7) that they became widely accepted. Then the same technology that allowed guitarists to control synthesizers also allowed all other instrumentalists, and even vocalists, to do the same.

Although keyboard controlled synths dominate the electronic music scene, guitar, drum, and other controllers continue to carve an important niche. **Guitar synthesizers** fall into two basic but similar categories, both of which rely on polyphonic pickups (also known as hex pickups because they read all six strings) to translate a guitar string's vibration into electronic information. **Proprietary systems** take the signal generated by the hex pickup and use it to drive an internal sound engine. These generally offer excellent tracking (the ability to accurately trigger a synth sound from the note being played). **MIDI**

systems take that same signal and convert it to MIDI note information, which is then fed to external devices such as synthesizers, samplers, and sequencers. Many of the proprietary devices offer some form of MIDI output, though you'll often notice a slight delay (lag) between the note being struck and the triggering of the MIDI device.

It seems that some players want to take advantage of every available part of the body in controlling the synthesizer. So foot controllers are also made, and they range from simple on-off pedals similar to the sustain pedal on a piano to full control panels for the feet — often used by guitar synthesists. There are also pedal keyboard controllers, similar to the bass pedals on organs.

Electronic Drums have also come a long way in recent years. Drum pads are effective triggers for sampled sounds (triggers can even be mounted on conventional acoustic drums). **Physical modeling** technology (see Chapter 4) has also emerged in electronic drumming as a means of bringing more expression to the drummer's performance.

Other Elements

In addition to the voltage-controlled oscillator, which produces simple waveforms, most analog synthesizers include a **noise generator**. This produces sound without any specific frequency, or, more precisely, sound in which all frequencies are present in equal amounts. It is useful in creating many special effects that would otherwise be impossible to produce. This noise, which sounds something like radio static, is also called "white noise." When it is filtered to emphasize or eliminate certain frequencies, the result is "colored noise."

Some synthesizers use technology to help play themselves. One component used for this purpose is the **arpeggiator**, which, when more than one note is being played at one time, causes the notes to sound one after the other (an arpeggio) rather than simultaneously. A related device, the sequencer, is discussed in Chapter 6.

Voices

There is sometimes confusion about the word "voice" as it is applied to synthesizers. Synthesizer designers prefer to use the word to describe the "polyphony" of an instrument: a 16-voice instrument is one that can play 16 notes at one time, for example. On the other hand, players often use it as a synonym for "patch" — a specific sound. To avoid confusion, it might be best to use "patch," or its equivalents, "preset" and "program," when talking about sounds.

Most synthesizers are able to play more than one patch at a time. These instruments are known as **polytimbral**, or **multitimbral**. The simplest of these play one patch in one part of the keyboard and another in the other part. These are known as **split** keyboards. On some, the player can determine where one patch stops and another starts; these instruments are said to have a **programmable split point**. Some keyboards can be split into more than two parts.

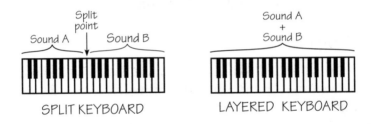

Just as a **split** keyboard plays different patches on different keys, a **layered** keyboard plays different patches on the same keys, at the same time. This allows the synthesist to play more than one "instrument" at the same time. Often, two versions of a single patch are layered, with one of them **detuned** — tuned slightly higher or lower than normal; the result is a fuller sound.

The most powerful aspect of a multitimbral instrument is that it can trigger different voices across a number of MIDI channels (see Chapter 7). For example, you could have one channel play a piano sound, another a drum sound, and another a bass sound, all at the same time. This feature is commonly used in sequencing.

Microprocessor Control

As mentioned before, the earliest analog synthesizers were modular and produced different sounds by means of patch cords and the setting of numerous switches and dials. Such instruments are still being made and used, but in increasingly smaller numbers. The primary drawbacks to them are that it takes time to change from one sound to another and it is not always possible to produce the same sound twice in a row, since analog controls incorporate a degree of uncertainty.

These drawbacks were overcome for the first time in the late 1970s, when **microprocessors** were introduced to the synthesizer world. Microprocessors made synthesizers **programmable:** capable of making changes to patch settings easily, then storing those settings so that the entire patch could be recalled at the touch of a button. Today, when the synthesist makes a change to a patch, he or she is said to be **editing** it, or **programming** the synthesizer.

Some people refer to the microprocessor as the "CPU" ("Central Processing Unit"); others call it a "computer brain." However, the microprocessor by itself is not quite a complete computer. A **program**, which is simply a set of instructions, is necessary to tell the microprocessor what operations to perform. This program is stored in memory — usually a kind of memory that can't be changed, so the program can't accidentally be erased. This kind of memory is known as **ROM**. That acronym stands for "Read-Only Memory," meaning the microprocessor can only "read" instructions from it; it can't "write" any instructions into it.

Patches in a programmable synthesizer are stored in a kind of memory that *can* be changed. This kind of memory is properly called "read-write memory," because the microprocessor can both "read" from it and "write" to it. It is more popularly known as **RAM** ("Random-Access Memory") because RAM and ROM sound good together. RAM requires electrical power to retain what is stored in it, so programmable synthesizers are equipped with a battery that serves as a backup power supply when the synthesizer itself is turned off.

Many synthesizers allow patches to be stored outside the instrument. This storage allows the player to assemble a "library" of sounds, more than could possibly fit in his instrument at one time. Depending on the instrument, storage may be on floppy disk, removable hard disk, CD-ROM, or a RAM cartridge that can be plugged into the instrument. Instruments that use RAM cartridges usually also have ROM cartridges available, containing patches that have been developed for commercial sale. Patches can also be stored on a computer via MIDI.

Because microprocessors deal with numbers, the adjective *digital* is frequently used when speaking of the things they do. The digital world — the world inside the computer — is a world of discrete divisions and separate steps. A digital clock, which contains a simple microprocessor, displays the time as definite numbers. In contrast, the analog world — the world around us — is a world of continuous change. An analog clock — the familiar one with the circular face and the sweeping second hand — shows not only the hours, minutes, and seconds, but all of the infinite times in between them. An analog synthesizer typically uses continuous controls (called "potentiometers," or "pots") to provide settings for the oscillators, filter, and so on. When programmability (microprocessor control) is added to such an instrument, the settings must be converted into numbers for storage in RAM. The result is a loss of the subtlety of continuous control but a gain in precision and the ability to reproduce a patch exactly.

4.
HOW DOES *DIGITAL SYNTHESIS WORK?*

ALMOST ALL ELECTRONIC MUSICAL DEVICES manufactured today — instruments, recorders, and effects — are digital. At one time, a "digital" synth was a sonic and technical alternative to an analog synth. Each used a very different method to create sound. Today, however, many analog-type sounds are available in digital form.

A purely digital synthesizer puts the microprocessor in charge of virtually every aspect of control. The difference between this kind of instrument and an analog one is the way the sounds are generated. A digital synthesizer begins with a series of numbers rather than an actual electrical wave. These numbers, which are stored in memory, *represent* a wave. Each number represents the amplitude — the height — of the wave at a certain point in its cycle. The microprocessor is responsible for reading the numbers from memory, one by one, and then sending them out to be assembled into a wave. The speed at which the numbers are sent out determines the frequency of the wave. This is the digital counterpart to the voltage-controlled oscillator, and in fact some digital instruments use the label "DCO" ("Digitally Controlled Oscillator").

At some point, the numbers must be translated into voltages, for it is electrical current that runs a loudspeaker, allowing the synthesized sounds to be heard. This is accomplished by a **digital-to-analog converter**, or **DAC**.

Since the numbers that the digital synthesizer uses to represent a wave are separate, discrete steps, and since they are produced at separate, discrete intervals of time, the output of the digital-to-analog converter resembles a staircase, rather than the smooth, continuous motion of the analog synthesizer.

Just as a digital wave looks different than an analog wave, it also sounds different. The sharp corners of the "steps" result in additional high harmonics. The easiest way to remove those harmonics is with a filter. This "smooths out" the wave.

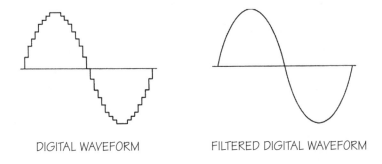

DIGITAL WAVEFORM   FILTERED DIGITAL WAVEFORM

Digital synthesis is not limited to the simple waveforms of analog synthesis. Producing different waveforms is simply a matter of generating different combinations of numbers.

Algorithms

There are many different methods of digital synthesis and it seems that instruments employing "new and improved" methods appear every year. These different methods are sometimes called **algorithms**, a word that means roughly the same thing as "procedure," or "recipe." What follows is a discussion of the most prominent of these.

Wave-table synthesis relies on lists, or **tables**, of numbers stored in memory. Each table contains the numeric representation of a different waveform. To generate a given waveform, the microprocessor sends out the numbers from the appropriate table.

Some wave-table synthesizers seek to unite the advantages of digital and analog filters.

Additive synthesis, also called **harmonic** synthesis, produces different timbres by combining (adding) waves at various pitches and volumes. Each of these waves represents a single harmonic.

Additive synthesis is also known as **Fourier synthesis**, after the 19th-century French physicist who first discovered that complex waves can be described as combinations of simple waves. Sophisticated applications of additive synthesis allow the simple waves to change independently over time — not only in volume, but in some cases, in pitch as well. Such instruments place a high degree of expressive control at the synthesist's disposal, but require an equally high degree of skill to program, not to mention a great deal of time.

Another algorithm of digital synthesis, which may be called additive in a more general sense of the word, involves combining two or more **complex** waveforms. Changes in timbre result from changes in the relative volumes of the component waves.

FM (frequency modulation) synthesis is a widely used algorithm for digital synthesis. The idea of frequency modulation was introduced in Chapter 2, with the example of a low-frequency oscillator modulating an audio-frequency oscillator. When the frequency of the modulating wave (the low-frequency wave) is below the audible range of 20Hz, the result is vibrato — a wavering of pitch.

But when the frequency of the modulating wave is raised into the audible range, it affects the timbre (the waveform), rather than the pitch, of the wave being modulated. The standard term for the modulating wave in FM synthesis is **modulator**. **Carrier** is the term for the wave being modulated.

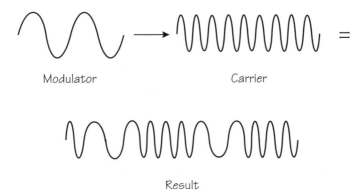

Modulator   Carrier

Result

Both additive synthesis and FM synthesis are possible on analog synthesizers, but benefit from the precise control available on digital instruments.

Waveshaping synthesis, also known as **nonlinear distortion** synthesis, is another useful digital algorithm. In this algorithm, a simple wave is "distorted," or "bent," into a different waveform.

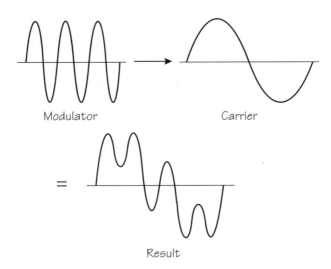

Modulator   Carrier

Result

Physical Modeling

While **physical modeling** isn't exactly new technology, its implementation in popular and affordable synthesizers (both hardware and computer driven) is. Modeling differs from other forms of sound generation because it involves creating a software model of a sound-producing element, such as a string, reed, or analog synth oscillator. Instead of simply taking a wave generated by an oscillator and using filters and amplifiers to modify its sound, modeling instruments work by digitally emulating the behavior and conditions associated with a sound. Thanks to recent increases in the computing power that drives DSP, modeling technology has become widely available in synthesizers, electronic drums, guitar amps and synths, effects devices, and more.

Instead of using the normal set of "electronic" instrument parameters, digital models refer to real life components of the device being modeled. For example, a guitar model might include information about the type of pickup, its position on the neck and more — the same terminology you'd use to describe a real guitar.

Sample Playback Synths

The most popular types of electronic instruments combine several different sound-shaping elements. **Sample playback** devices (also known as PCM-based devices) use samples as the framework of their sound. This technology, which first appeared in the late 1980's, continues to be the basis of many of today's General MIDI (GM) devices and high-end workstations. Most of these instruments store a bank of samples (short digital recordings) in memory. These can be traditional acoustic timbres or more exotic electronic fare and rhythmic loops. The samples are then processed by the instrument's electronics — using the types of filters and envelopes described in Chapter 2. (For more on sampling, see Chapter 5.)

Many of the higher-end sample playback instruments also allow the user to record their own samples or load them from third-party libraries. Some models also allow sample-derived sounds to play alongside FM sounds, modeled analog-type patches, and other electronic-type timbres. Instruments that offer multitimbral operation with a built-in sequencer are often referred to as workstations. Many of these are based around sample-playback synths.

Software Synths

In truth, all digital synthesizers are software-based. The thing that gives an individual instrument its sonic personality is largely a function of proprietary software burned into the unit's memory banks. The category of **software synthesis**, however, refers to something else — synthesizers that exist on a personal computer and create sounds with the computer's processing power and built-in audio capabilities instead of using any hardware of its own.

Software synths have exploded in popularity and cover a wide gamut, from emulations of old drum machines to samplers to programs that behave like large modular synthesizers to combinations of all of the above. Because they're not restricted by hardware limitations, many software-based instruments offer advantages in power and flexibility over their hardware counterparts.

Many of these devices can be controlled with third-party recording software via MIDI and can output their audio directly to digital recording software.

Computer Based Hardware Synths

Unlike software synths, these instruments *do* have their own electronic components, but rather than being packaged in keyboards or rack modules, they reside on a card that can be installed in a personal computer. The computer controls the "front-end" interface. These come in a variety of forms, from the simple hardware found in many consumer-level soundcards, to more elaborate professional samplers, synthesizers, and devices that combine some forms of synthesis with digital recording.

Different kinds of synthesizers are good for producing different kinds of sounds. Analog synthesizers are known for producing "warm, fat" sounds. Digital synthesizers excel in creating "clean, sharp" sounds. You can choose to play several different kinds of synthesizers in order to have different kinds of sounds available at all times.

5.

WHY IS DIGITAL SAMPLING SO POPULAR?

FOR MANY PEOPLE, the sounds of acoustic instruments are more satisfying than those of synthesizers. They are the sounds they grew up with, so they are more familiar. In addition, they are inherently more interesting than many electronic sounds because they are more complex and capable of greater variety.

On the other hand, electronic instruments offer several advantages, such as stability of tuning, portability, low price, and connection to sequence recorders for note-perfect performances (see Chapter 6).

Some new musical instruments seek to unite the benefits of acoustic sounds and electronic control. The primary means of doing so is **digital sampling,** often merely called "sampling." Sampling can be understood as the digital recording of a sound. This is essentially the reverse of the production of a sound in a digital synthesizer:

The sound starts in the real world as a sound wave. It is converted to an electrical wave by a microphone. The amplitude (height) of this wave is measured at regular intervals of time. Each of these measurements is called a **sample** (although, by extension, the entire sampled sound is often referred to as a sample, too). These sampled electrical voltages are converted to numbers by an **analog-to-digital converter (ADC).** The numbers are then stored in memory.

The numbers can be turned back into sound by exactly the same method that digital synthesizers use: a digital-to-analog converter changes the numbers to voltages, then a filter smooths the rough edges, and finally an amplifier and speaker system convert the electrical current into sound.

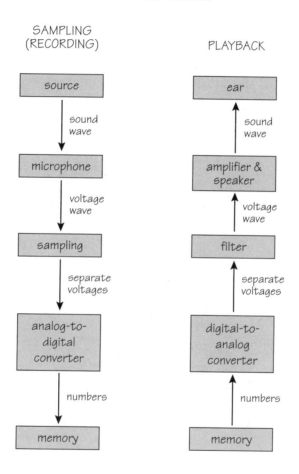

Multi-Sampling

It would seem that, as in digital synthesis, one sampled sound could be made to generate an entire musical scale merely by being played back from memory at different speeds. Played back slowly, it would produce a low pitch; played back quickly, it would produce a high pitch. This is correct, as far as it goes. However, when reproducing the sounds of acoustic instruments, it fails to take an important fact into consideration. High and low acoustic sounds are not merely fast and slow versions of the same waveform.

For example, if you take a recording of a man singing and play it back twice as fast, it doesn't sound like a man singing an octave higher; it sounds like a chipmunk! In fact, this is how the many "chipmunk" recordings of the 1950s and 1960s were made. They used ordinary analog tape recordings, but the principle applies to digital sampling as well.

The way to overcome the "chipmunk effect" is to use samples of different pitches, rather than a single sample at different speeds, to construct a musical scale. This is known as **multi-sampling**. (It is usually not necessary nor practical to sample every pitch of the scale. To conserve memory, most multi-sampling instruments rely on a smaller number of samples, taken at different points in the scale, which are sped up and slowed down to produce the pitches in between.)

The "Chipmunk Effect": One sample does not fit all.

Another use of multi-sampling involves sounds of different dynamics. To use the familiar example of the piano, consider a single note being played twice — first softly, then loudly. The difference in sound is actually much more than just "soft" versus "loud." The softer tone is also more muted than the loud tone. Stated another way, the loud tone is brighter, has more high harmonics. In order to reproduce this kind of variety, samples taken at different dynamic levels are necessary.

Multi-sampling also allows samples of different keys, or even the same key. In this way, the sounds of flute, string orchestra, and guitar (for example) might be played from a single keyboard at one time.

Looping

An important technique for conserving memory, and hence cost, in a sampling instrument is **looping**. As the name suggests, this involves storing only a short segment of a sound, which is played over and over again when a long sound is called for, rather than recording the original sound in its entirety.

Samplers were originally designed to help capture these sounds, and their ability to do so is one reason for their popularity. Samplers are also extensively used for recording and playback of rhythmic audio loops, such as drum grooves, guitar riffs, and more. Today's breed of samplers offer enhanced tools designed to work with loops, such as time stretching, pitch-shifting, tempo calculation, and more.

Resynthesis

One of the shortcomings of sampling is that, unlike synthesis, the sound is fixed — it cannot be changed. This can be overcome, to some extent, by putting the sampled sound through filters, envelope generators, and such, but there are limits to what these add-ons can accomplish. "Wouldn't it be wonderful," you might say, "if I could start with the sounds of the real world, such as sampling provides, and then change anything about them, as I can with a synthesizer."

You have probably guessed by now that such a thing is not at all impossible. The solution lies in what is called **resynthesis.** What this means is that the sampled sound is analyzed by a computer and "translated" — resynthesized — into an algorithm of digital synthesis. Additive synthesis is the algorithm usually used. From this point, you can change any aspect of the sound, just as you can with any other sound constructed by additive synthesis. In a sense, resynthesis fulfills the promise made by sampling: the uniting of acoustic sounds and electronic control.

6.

WHAT DO ALL THOSE OTHER BOXES DO?

SYNTHESIZERS AND SAMPLING INSTRUMENTS are only the beginning of the equipment that is related to making music with the help of electronics. You can bring many other devices into play. The most fundamental of these are amplifiers and speakers, since many synthesizers do not have them built in. And if you play more than one electronic instrument at a time using a single sound system, you also need a **mixer** to combine the sounds. Many times small mixers are built into multitrack tape recorders, resulting in what amounts to a portable recording studio.

Effects

On the subject of sound, there are many different **effects** devices, sometimes called **signal-processing** devices, available to enhance the sound of the music you produce. **Reverberation,** or "reverb," adds a feeling of resonance to the sound, such as is produced in a concert hall. **Digital delay** is used for a variety of effects, including chorus (the illusion of several instruments playing the same part) and echo (different from reverb in that it consists of discrete repetitions of the sound; reverb is less distinct, more of a "wash" of sound).

Reverberation   Chorus   Echo

Equalizers allow you to emphasize or de-emphasize certain ranges of frequencies. They're essentially refinements of the "Bass" and "Treble" tone controls found on many home stereos. **Noise gates** cut out any sound below a certain level of volume. These are often used when recording with microphones, to eliminate background noise, but have a special application in contemporary music: When used in conjunction with reverb,

Gated Reverb

they produce a sound that is both resonant and "dry," since, when the reverberation descends to a certain level, it cuts off abruptly rather than trailing off naturally. The classic example of this gated reverb, as it is called, is the sound of Phil Collins's snare drum.

A **limiter** does the opposite of a noise gate: it cuts out sounds *above* a specified level of volume. A related device is the **compressor,** which "evens out" the overall volume by increasing the volume of soft sounds and decreasing the volume of loud ones.

Panning devices are used to cause the sound to shift back and forth between the right and left stereo channels. **Pitch transposers,** also called **pitch shifters** and **harmonizers,** can change the pitch of a note. They have a number of uses. When the pitch shift is slight, the shifted note and the original note can be combined for a thick detuned effect. The shift can also be to another note entirely, so that the original and shifted notes together produce two-part harmony. Some harmonizers are capable of producing harmony in several parts at one time.

The **vocoder** can make a musical instrument such as synthesizer "speak" or "sing." It does this by superimposing the timbre (the vowels and consonants) of a vocal sound onto the pitch or pitches of an instrumental sound.

Most modern effects units allow real-time control (either via MIDI or foot-controller) and are so powerful that they themselves sound like synthesizers.

Instruments

The separation of synthesizer keyboards from their sound-producing hardware, mentioned in Chapter 3, led to the commercial production of **remote keyboard controllers,** which produce no sound of their own, but rather are used to play external synthesizers. Some of these controllers are portable "strap-on" models, while others are full-size keyboards.

The remote keyboard led naturally to a complementary device, the **expander module,** or **tone module,** which is an electronic musical instrument "in a box" — that is, without a keyboard of its own. Many of these modules are made to be mounted in a standard rack designed for audio components.

Single height rack module

Part of the attractiveness of using electronic technology to make music lies in the ability to play things you wouldn't otherwise be able to play. This is the function of the **sequence recorder,** or **sequencer,** which is perhaps the cornerstone of the "democratization of music" mentioned at the beginning of this book.

When analog synthesizers were in their prime, a sequencer consisted of a bank of adjustable controls that could produce a repeating "sequence" of notes. Each control specified the pitch of a single note, and so the number of notes in the sequence was limited by the expense and impracticality of a large number of controls. With the introduction of microprocessors, the number of notes that the sequencers could produce expanded greatly, since the information for playing each note could now be stored in memory and no longer required a separate control for each note. Furthermore, these digital sequencers allow you to record directly from the synthesizer. Most offer a choice of recording in **step mode** (specifying each note individually) or in **real-time mode** (live).

With a sequencer you can record slowly and play back at a faster speed without changing the pitch, because you are re-cording **musical information** (note on, note off, etc.) rather than actual sounds. You can change patches during playback, if you wish. And if your sense of rhythm is less than perfect, you can use **quantization** to line everything up with the beats. Sequencers even allow you to perform "microsurgery" on your music, lengthening a note here, changing a pitch there.

Recorded sequence before quantization.

Same sequence after quantization.

Sequencers are available in both hardware and software forms. Today, software sequencers record MIDI and audio into a com-puter and offer a powerful arsenal of tracking and editing tools. Hardware sequencers can come in stand-alone units or, more commonly, as part of a keyboard or rhythm workstation and beatbox.

Remote keyboards, expander modules, and sequencers have mushroomed in popularity since the advent of MIDI (discussed in the next chapter), as have **drum machines.** A drum machine essentially combines a special sequencer and the electronics necessary to produce percussion sounds. Most drum machines use samples to generate these sounds. These units have always been a staple of electronic music. Modern **beat boxes** have taken the simple concept of pattern-based rhythm programming much further than the original breed of unnatural-sounding drum machines. These units combine drum programming, sampling, and sequencing. They can work with single samples or looped rhythm patterns and allow for extensive real-time control over parameters such as speed, pitch, envelope, and more.

7.

WHAT IS MIDI?

IN 1981, DAVE SMITH, President of Sequential Circuits, delivered a proposal at the convention of the Audio Engineering Society for what he called the Universal Synthesizer Interface (USI). This proposal was based on discussion among several manufacturers of electronic musical instruments. Further discussion and modification of the proposal resulted in an agreement in 1982 for what is now called **Musical Instrument Digital Interface**, or **MIDI**. The details were ironed out by 1983, when the "MIDI 1.0 Specification" was published. It was the birth of a new era in music, considered by many to be as important as the development of the analog synthesizer in the mid-1960s.

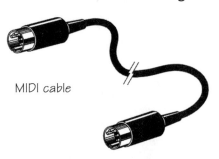

MIDI cable

MIDI is the glue that holds modern musical electronics together. "Interface," means "connection." It also means communication. What MIDI does is allow instruments made by different manufacturers to "talk" to one another. In fact, the original purpose of MIDI was simply to allow two synthesizers to be connected so that you could press a key on one and have both instruments play. That it does, and much more, as you'll find out. But before discussing what MIDI does, let's take a look at what it is.

What MIDI Is

On the surface, MIDI is easy to define: it consists of cables that plug into musical instruments and related equipment. The standard MIDI cable has a five-pin plug on each end. These plugs fit into what are called MIDI **ports.** There are three different ports possible (though not all MIDI equipment has all three), labeled IN, OUT, and THRU:

- IN receives MIDI information from other equipment.

- OUT sends MIDI information to other equipment.

- THRU provides a duplicate of the information received by IN, to be passed along to other equipment.

IN   OUT   THRU

MIDI ports

The "MIDI 1.0 Spec," as it's called, gives requirements for the electronics hardware necessary to make MIDI work as well as outlining the MIDI language. That language consists of numbers (remember: **digital** interface) that can be interpreted and acted upon by the microprocessors in electronic musical instruments.

What MIDI Does

The simplest use of MIDI is to control a synthesizer remotely. To do this, a MIDI cable is used to connect the OUT port of one synthesizer to the IN port of another. This is called a "master-slave" setup.

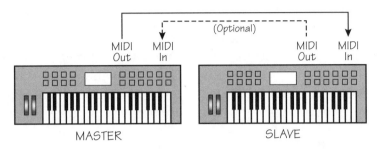

A master-slave setup

Playing the keyboard of the "master" will cause the "slave" to sound as well. It is important to re-emphasize that what is sent over the MIDI cable is **information (data)**, not sound. In fact, the usefulness of this kind of setup lies in having each instrument produce a different sound, resulting in a true instrumental ensemble.

A MIDI master-slave setup can also consist of a remote keyboard controller and an expander module, or a sequencer and a synthesizer or other MIDI-equipped instrument. For the purposes of both recording and playback with a sequencer, the IN and OUT ports of both units are used:

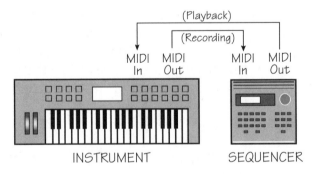

A two-way master-slave setup

Using the THRU port of the slave allows more slaves to be added in series. This is known as **daisy-chaining**:

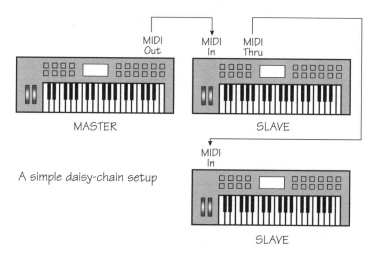

A simple daisy-chain setup

But daisy-chaining is not without problems; after two or three slaves, the MIDI information can undergo some distortion, with the result that further slaves in the chain may not play accurately. The solution to this lies in the use of a **MIDI THRU box**, or **multiport MIDI interface**, which produces several parallel THRU signals from one IN:

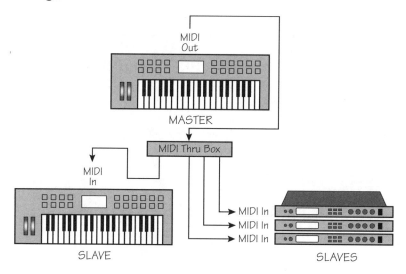

Master-slave connections using MIDI Thru

Picture this: You've recorded an entire symphony into a MIDI sequencer and have connected a dozen slaves to play the parts — synthesizers, sampling instruments, expander modules, electronic pianos, electronic organs, and portable keyboards. Everything's plugged in, turned on, and ready to run. In nervous anticipation, you press START on the sequencer and all your instruments start to play. But wait! They're all playing the same part!

Clearly, MIDI sequencing would be severely limited if there weren't some way of directing different parts to different instruments. The authors of the specification foresaw this, and included such a means of separation: MIDI **channels.**

MIDI channels can be compared to TV channels: an instrument has to be "tuned" to the correct one or it won't receive what is being transmitted. There are 16 channels available and each one can transmit any number of notes to any number of instruments. To return to our example of the symphony, you could record the flute part on channel 1, and set an appropriate sampling instrument to that channel for playback. If the string parts

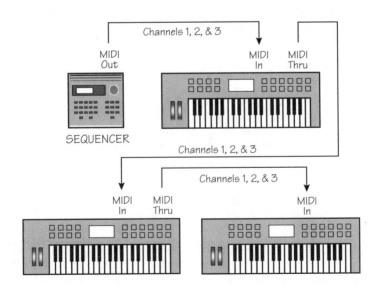

MIDI channels

were on channel 2, you might set three different expander modules to that channel, detuning them slightly for a fuller sound and setting one to play an octave higher than the others. If the trombone part, using the pitch bend control for its many slides, were on channel 3, you could set a synthesizer to that channel with the appropriate patch, and so on. Any or all MIDI channels can be transmitted over a single MIDI cable.

Multiport MIDI interfaces, which are especially useful when a computer is part of the equation, allow you to assign each port its own cable, with each cable able to carry 16 char   of MIDI information. Thus, an 8-port interface can offer 1   rate channels of MIDI. Although some multiport interf be chained together, offering the potential for hundred channels, their more important benefit is that they c instrument in a MIDI studio to have its own connection computer (doing away with thru lines and patch-boxes). This improves timing and makes it easier to edit individual instruments using the computer. Combining MIDI sequencers and instruments amounts to having a tapeless recording studio!

There is one more item to include in a discussion of channels: a thing called **Omni** mode. Omni mode means that the instrument in question will receive on all MIDI channels at the same time. (Note that Omni mode involves receiving MIDI information; nothing *transmits* in Omni mode.) Some instruments cannot be sent to Omni mode; others cannot be set to anything else.

General MIDI

General MIDI is a specification that enhances compatibility between various MIDI devices. One of the major advantages of GM is that it provides standardization of sound and channel assignments. This allows a sequence such as a Standard MIDI File (SMF) to play back correctly on any GM device without any further adjustment from the user. Many synths are either completely GM-compatible or offer GM sound-sets.

More Than Notes

From what has been said about Omni mode you can see that, although MIDI is a standard, different instruments *implement* it to different degrees. How do you know what areas of the specification a MIDI-compatible piece of equipment does and doesn't implement? Read the **MIDI Implementation Chart** that comes with it. Every piece of MIDI equipment has one of these.

MIDI information covers much more than just "note on, note off." Provisions have been made for velocity and after-touch information, used by touch-sensitive keyboards. Most instruments include recognition of MIDI **program changes,** so that when you activate patch number 5 on the master, patch number 5 on the slave will also be activated. (Once again, it is not the **sound** that is transmitted. For example, on the master, number 5 might be a synthesized piano sound, while on the slave it might be a sample of a quacking duck.) Pitch bend is another area of the specification, as are controllers, such as the sustain pedal and mod wheel.

MIDI sequencers and drum machines can synch together so that two separate units can play back in time with one another. Methods include MIDI Clocks and, in some cases MIDI Time Code (MTC), which can also be used for locking a sequencer to a tape machine that has been "striped" with time code.

Equipment other than musical instruments is also MIDI-compatible. Audio effects devices and mixers are one prominent category. There are also MIDI lighting controllers.

System Exclusive

There were precedents for MIDI in interfacing systems developed previously by several synthesizer manufacturers (in fact, modular synthesizers, by definition, required communication among several units), but these worked only with equipment of one given brand. As mentioned before, the idea behind MIDI is communication between instruments of a given brand to be

MIDI Implementation Chart

Manufacturer:_____ Model:_____ Version:_____ Date:_____

Function		Transmitted	Recognized	Remarks
Basic Channel	Default Changed			
Mode	Default Messages			
Note Number	True Voice			
Velocity	Note ON			
	Note OFF			
After Touch	Keys Channels			
Pitch Bender				
Control Change				
Bank Select				
Program Change	True No.			
All Sound Off				
All Notes Off				
Reset all Controllers				
System Exclusive				
System Common	:Song Pos :Song Sel :Tune			
System Real Time	:Clock :Cmnds			
Aux Msgs	:Local On/off :Active Sense :Reset			

NOTES:
Mode 1: Omni ON, Poly   Mode 2: Omni ON, Mono
Mode 3: Omni OFF, Poly   Mode 4: Omni OFF, Mono

able to exchange information that pertained only to that brand or that model. They allowed for this in MIDI by a capability called **system exclusive.**

System exclusive information is used mostly to transmit patch settings (or sampled waveforms) between instruments. It also is used to "dump" the memory contents of one sequencer (or drum machine) to another of the same kind. And it has applications in some computer programs designed to work with specific instruments.

The Computer Connection

The digital messages of MIDI are made to order for personal computers, which contain microprocessors just as electronic musical instruments do. So it should come as no surprise that in addition to the **computer-based synthesizers** discussed in Chapter 4, a great number of MIDI products have to do with computers.

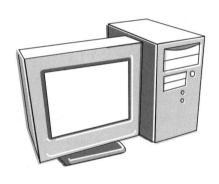

THE COMPUTER
The ultimate MIDI device?

Two things are necessary for a computer to "speak MIDI." The first of these is the proper interface. Yes, you're right, MIDI *is* an interface, but since most computers don't have MIDI ports built in (a few do), they require some sort of adapter (an interface, in other words), to connect to MIDI cables. The second thing necessary is the proper software. The personal computer can't do anything at all until it is told what to do and how to do it. There are several kinds of MIDI software available for personal computers:

Patch librarians allow you to assemble a "library" of sounds for your synthesizer. The patches are transferred between synthesizer and computer using system exclusive information.

Patches can be arranged and rearranged easily with the advantage of being able to see them listed on the computer screen. (The screen is one of the most important assets of the personal computer, since it shows more information than the displays in most "dedicated" musical instruments can.)

Patch editors, or **voicing programs,** allow you to edit voices with the help of the computer. Again, system exclusive information makes it possible; and again, the screen makes the job easier than it would otherwise be. Some of these programs go so far as to "invent" new patches for you.

Waveform editors are the equivalent of patch editors for sampling instruments. Waveforms can be cut, spliced, looped, redrawn, and more.

Computer-based sequencers are among the most powerful tools on the musical scene. Most of today's programs offer a combination of MIDI and digital audio recording, and many can interface with hardware and software synths and samplers at the same time. Software sequencers with MIDI Machine Control capabilities can be used to control outboard tape recorders, and some of the leading programs also work directly with editor/librarian software, allowing complete control over every element of the studio from one central location.

Music printing (scoring) programs give you "sheet music" capabilities from the computer printer. Often these, too, work with a software sequencer.

Education programs are available as well, covering all aspects of music, from "What is a treble clef?" to "Trumpet fingering."

Where do we go from here?

PREDICTIONS ARE ALWAYS DANGEROUS. No one knows for certain what technological marvels await the musician of the future. In years to come, we can expect that electronic instruments will become easier to use and produce better sound; price-to-performance ratios will continue to become more attractive; computers will play an increasing role in music making; and sounds will be shared over the Internet.

But, despite all the change and uncertainty, one thing will remain constant: Music will always be a means for people to express themselves. For you, that may mean writing a computer program that composes music by itself; it may mean strumming a guitar and singing folk songs; it may mean MIDIing two portable keyboards together and playing Broadway show tunes.

It is *not* necessary to have the latest technology to make satisfying, expressive music. The piano is several hundred years old and remains a superlative musical instrument. True, technology can help. If you play the guitar but dream of having an orchestra at your disposal, MIDI is for you. If you want to play music but you're all thumbs, sequencers are for you. If you'd like to practice the drums but don't want to disturb your neighbors, electronic drums are for you. Just remember: The pieces of equipment are only tools. What is most important is *you*. Make music! Express yourself! There is no substitute for that, and there never will be.

GLOSSARY

Audio File: A digital recording that has been saved to hard disk. Common formats include .wav, AIFF, and .sd2.

Drum Machine: A device that can be used to create and play back electronic drum sounds created by *samples* stored inside the machine.

General MIDI: A standard that specifies sound and controller assignments, voice allocation, and other aspects of the operation of compatible MIDI instruments.

Master: A MIDI device that controls others.

MIDI: Musical Instrument Digital Interface, a serial connection that allows compatible instruments to communicate with one another.

MIDI Clocks and Song Position Pointer: MIDI timing messages that allow MIDI devices to synchronize based on tempo and song position.

MIDI Machine Control: System Exclusive messages that can be used to remotely control tape and hard disk recorders.

MIDI Time Code: A combination of MIDI timing and system exclusive (Sysex) messages that allows MIDI devices to synchronize to absolute time.

Monophonic: A monophonic instrument can play one note or voice at a time. Many polyphonic instruments can have one or more voices play back in "mono" mode.

Multitimbral: A multitimbral instrument can play more than one voice (or sound) independently. Each sound is played back on its own MIDI channel. Multitimbral instruments are especially useful with sequencers.

Polyphonic/Polyphony: A polyphonic instrument can play more than one voice at a time. Polyphony refers to the number of voices available: for example, a synth with 16-voice polyphony can play 16 voices at one time.

Sampler: An electronic instrument that uses digital recordings to create life-like sounds.

Sequencer: A device for the recording, editing, and playback of MIDI information.

Slave: A MIDI device that is controlled by others.

Standard MIDI File: A sequence file format that can be exchanged between devices of different types and manufacturers.

Synthesizer: An instrument that generates sound by the creation and manipulation of artificial waveforms.

INDEX

additive synthesis, 29, 30, 38
ADSR, 14
after-touch (pressure), 17, 20, 50
algorithms, 28–30, 38
amplitude, 7–9, 17, 27, 34
amplitude modulation, 17
analog synthesizers, 3, 11–18, 26, 27–33, 41–42
analogs, 12
analog-to-digital converter, 34
arpeggiator, 23
Attack, 14
audio file, 55

beatboxes, 42, 43

Carlos, Wendy, 1
carrier, 30
channel controller, 17
"chipmunk effect," 36
chorus, 39–40
Collins, Phil, 40
compressor, 40
computers, 32–33, 52–53
continuous controllers, 17, 26
control voltages, 15
controllers, 12, 20–23, 50
cycles, 5–6

daisy-chaining, 47
decibel (dB), 8–9
Delay, 14
detuning, 24
digital, 26, 45
digital delay, 39
digital synthesizers, 3, 12, 20, 27, 33
digitally controlled oscillator, 27
digital-to-analog converter, 27–28, 35
drum machines, 43, 50, 52, 55
dynamics, 37
echo, 39–40
editing, 25
education programs, 53
effects, 39–41, 50
electronic drums, 23, 54
envelope generator, 14–15, 16, 18, 20, 37

envelopes, 13–15, 31
equalizers, 40
expander module, 41, 46, 49

filter modulation, 17
filters, 31, 35, 37
foot controllers, 17, 23, 41
Fourier synthesis, 29
frequency, 5–7, 8, 17
frequency modulation synthesis, 29–30

gate, 15, 18
General MIDI, 31, 49, 55
glide, 21
guitar controllers, 22

Hammer, Jan, 22
Hammond organ, 19, 20
hardware sequencers, 42
harmonic synthesis, 29
harmonics (overtones), 10, 16
harmonizers, 40
Hertz (Hz), 6, 8, 29

keyboards, 2, 12, 20–22, 24, 41, 42, 46
layered keyboard, 24
left-hand controllers, 21
limiter, 40
looping, 37
low-frequency oscillator, 16–17, 18, 29
Lyricon, 21

master, 45–47, 55
memory, 25–26, 27, 32, 52
microphones, 34, 40
microprocessors, 25–26, 27, 42, 52
MIDI, 22–23, 41, 44–53, 54, 55
MIDI cables, 44, 45, 49, 52
MIDI channels, 48–49
MIDI Clocks, 50
MIDI Implementation Chart, 50, 51
MIDI IN, 45
MIDI lighting controllers, 50
MIDI Machine Control, 53, 55
MIDI OUT, 45
MIDI ports, 45, 52
MIDI program changes, 50

MIDI specification, 44, 45
MIDI THRU, 45, 47
MIDI THRU box, 47–49
MIDI Time Code, 50, 55
MIDI Timing Clock, 55
mixers, 39, 50
modular synthesizers, 11, 19
modulation, 16–17
modulation wheel, 17, 18, 50
modulator, 30
monophonic mode, 21, 55
monophonic synthesizers, 12–13
Moog synthesizer, 1
multiport MIDI interface, 47–49
multi-sampling, 35–37
multitimbral instruments, 24–25, 55
music printing programs, 53
noise gates, 40
noise generator, 23
nonlinear distortion synthesis, 30

Omni mode, 49, 50
oscilloscope, 5, 7, 9

panning devices, 40
patch editors, 53
patch librarians, 26, 52–53
patches, 11, 24–26, 49, 50, 52–53
PCM-based devices, 31–32
pedal keyboard controllers, 23
physical modeling, 3, 23, 31
pitch, 4, 5–7, 12–13
pitch bend, 21, 22, 49, 50
pitch transposers (shifters), 40
polyphonic pickups, 22
polyphonic synthesizers, 12–13, 24
polyphony, 55
portamento, 21
potentiometers, 26
programmable split point, 24
programmable synthesizers, 25–26
proprietary systems, 22, 32

quantization, 42

RAM, 26
real-time control, 41
real-time mode, 42
Release, 14
remote keyboard controllers, 41
resynthesis, 37–38
reverberation, 39–40

Rhodes electric piano, 19, 20
ROM, 25–26

sample playback synthesizers, 31–32
samplers, sampling, 3, 31–32, 34–38, 55
sequencers, 23, 41–43, 46, 50, 52, 53, 54, 55
signal-processing devices, 39
slaves, 45–47, 55
software, 52–53
software sequencers, 42, 53
software synthesis, 32
Song Position Pointer, 55
sound waves, 4–8, 34
soundcards, 33
split keyboards, 24
Standard MIDI Files, 49, 55
step mode, 42
"strap-on" keyboard controllers, 22, 41
subtractive synthesis, 16
Sustain, 14
sustain pedal, 50
Switched-On Bach, 1
synthesizer defined, 3, 55
system exclusive information, 50, 52–53
timbre, 4, 9–10, 15–16, 40–41
tone module. See expander module
tremolo, 17
trigger, 15, 18

velocity, 20, 50
vibrato (frequency modulation), 17, 29
vocoder, 40–41
voices, 24–25
voicing programs, 53
voltage-controlled amplifier, 13, 15, 17, 18
voltage-controlled filter, 16, 17, 18
voltage-controlled oscillator, 12, 15, 17, 18, 23, 27, 29
volume, 4, 7–9, 13–15

waveform, 9–10
waveform editors, 53
waveshaping synthesis, 30
wave-table synthesis, 28–29
"white noise," 23
wind controllers, 21

ABOUT THE AUTHORS

JON F. EICHE has served as an editor and writer for Hal Leonard Corporation since 1980. He has worked on owner's manuals and other books for Yamaha, Casio, Roland, Kurzweil, and other manufacturers of electronic musical instruments. He's also covered another side of plugged-in music: guitar gear, including books about Fender, Marshall, Ampeg, and other brands.

A keyboardist, songwriter, and Chapman Stick player, he frequently applies his knowledge of musical technology in performances at church with his wife, a singer.

EMILE MENASCHÉ is a writer, editor, composer, and producer living in the New York metro area.